OX

Chinese Horoscope 2025

By
IChingHunFùyŏu FengShuisu

Table of Contents

Introduce

The character of people born in the year of the OX

You're honest and calm, and don't act rashly because of gossip or trivia. When you meditate until your thoughts become crystallized. You'll start acting and, while carrying out various tasks, you should proceed with caution. You could go on and on, but you never give up easily, so when someone is a steer and rushes ahead of you at first, they are all panting. In the end, you'll be able to score game-changing goals. You must give excitement to another zodiac sign if you choose excitement. If you want to be certain, it's someone born in the year of the bull. You know exactly what you want.

People born this year have a lot of patience and decisiveness. A decision is made without hesitation. Say the words: high responsibility, honesty. When he is angry, he has a strong temper, anger, dislikes making friends with others, is not social, prefers to live alone, has excellent intelligence, a strong heart, and regards art as his life. People born in this year are frequently bad at business. They are best suited for careers in government or medicine. In addition, the person born this year is another person with whom to be in a relationship.

Strength:
A person with a stable mind who is reliant on others adores brothers and sisters.

Weaknesses:
 Life is frequently fraught with peril.

Love:
People born in this year are more likely to experience romantic love. When you love someone, you treasure them. Love is like a magnifying glass. The first rule of love is honesty. The thrill of love is often gradual and not flashy for the young man born in the year of the cow. But it's quite tasty. As a result, the love of those born this year is frequently long-lasting. People born this year may appear quiet on the surface, but they are not inferior to

anyone else. This story will keep you hooked on the love of the Ox for a long time.

Suitable Career:

People born in the year of the Ox are considered to be of the earth element. Should pursue a career in soil, agriculture, or real estate, such as land brokering, building a dormitory or condominium for rent, or working in a hotel. Department stores, opening a shop selling jewelry, gems, jade, stones, ceramics, various ores, and so on, building materials stores, or working in the Department of Mineral Resources drilling minerals are all possibilities.

Year of the OX (Fire) | (1937) & (1997)

"The OX in the stall" is a person born in the year of the OX at the age of 88 years (1937) and 28 years (1997)

Overview

Seniors aged 88 years old, because the planets that orbit into your horoscope house this year are "Dangerous Star", "Moon" and "Blue Dog Star", which all three stars will spread their influence and cause arguments with others easily. However, seniors should let go and avoid interfering in personal matters and family matters of their children and grandchildren so that they do not have to worry. In addition, the person needs to be careful of health problems, especially latent diseases that often appear quietly, and be careful of accidents of slipping and falling.

For the person aged 28 years old, because the planets that orbit into your horoscope house this year are "Sharp Sword Star" and other minor auspicious stars.

On the positive side, this year is good for you to receive auspicious energy to support your career, which will progress as you wish. For those who do business, it will be smooth and prosperous. Therefore, you should be determined and develop yourself often because your perseverance will not be in vain. Your work will be noticeable to your elders, which means you will have the opportunity to be promoted, including increased compensation, or be able to expand your income into increased sales. Therefore, please use your knowledge, abilities, and intelligence to work hard to the fullest. However, on the bad side, the person must be careful of being envied, being bullied by people who try to harm them until it becomes an endless dispute. Therefore, please be patient and do not risk retaliation by exchanging your body. Then everything will be as good as you think.

Career and Business

This year, your career horoscope shows a path of progress. Therefore, you should seize this opportunity to work hard to create results and expand your income. Do not let smooth times pass without doing anything significant. Especially during the months when your career and business are heading in a good direction, namely, the 12th Chinese month (January 5 – February 2), the 2nd Chinese month (March 5 – April 3), the 7th Chinese month (August 7 – September 6), and the 10th Chinese month (November 7 – December 6). Furthermore, these months are suitable for starting a new job, entering into a joint venture, or investing in new businesses. You will see the results in return as beautiful numbers at the end of the year.

As for the months when your work or business will encounter problems and obstacles, they are the 3rd Chinese month (April 4 - May 4), the 6th Chinese month (July 7 - August 6), the 9th Chinese month (October 8 - November 6), and the 11th Chinese month (December 7, 2024 - January 4, 2025). Do not be greedy for other people's wealth. Be careful not to be tricked into losing your wealth. Also, you should be careful about making contracts during this period, which requires more caution, because you may be at a disadvantage to others.

Financial

This year, your career horoscope shows a path of progress. Therefore, you should seize this opportunity to work hard to create results and expand your income. Do not let smooth times pass without doing anything significant. Especially during the months when your career and business are heading in a good direction, namely, the 12th Chinese month (January 5 – February 2), the 2nd Chinese month (March 5 – April 3), the 7th Chinese month (August 7 – September 6), and the 10th Chinese month (November 7 – December 6). Furthermore, these months are suitable for starting a new job, entering into a joint venture, or investing in new businesses. You will see the results in return as beautiful numbers at the end of the year.

As for the months when your work or business will encounter problems and obstacles, they are the 3rd Chinese month (April 4 - May 4), the

6th Chinese month (July 7 - August 6), the 9th Chinese month (October 8 - November 6), and the 11th Chinese month (December 7, 2025 - January 4, 2026). Do not be greedy for other people's wealth. Be careful not to be tricked into losing your wealth. Also, you should be careful about making contracts during this period, which requires more caution, because you may be at a disadvantage to others.

Family

This year, family events are both good and bad. The important thing is that you should increase your care and attention to the health of your family members, especially the elderly. In addition, be careful of juniors or subordinates in the house causing trouble, especially during bad months. Conflicts in the family can easily arise, such as the 3rd Chinese month (April 4 - May 4), the 6th Chinese month (July 7 - August 6), the 9th Chinese month (October 8 - November 6), and the 11th Chinese month (December 7, 2025 - January 4, 2026).

In addition, be careful of dangers from thieves. Be careful of the elderly in the house slipping and falling. However, this year, if your house can organize an auspicious event, such as a house blessing, a birthday blessing, or a wedding celebration, etc., it will be considered a way to resolve the bad luck and help dissolve the bad energy from the Tai Yin star and the Xiao Ae star, turning it into good. As for close friends and relatives, this year is good for support. The person will receive help and support in both their work, pioneering work, and new business ventures.

Love
The love aspect of both horoscopes this year is quite volatile due to the influence of the Tai Yin and Xiao Ae stars. This results in love not being smooth, and often having disagreements over trivial matters. Also, be careful that temporary love will destroy permanent love. Therefore, this year, the horoscope should avoid getting involved in family matters and love affairs of other couples, including avoiding going to entertainment venues. The months when your

love will easily have problems and arguments are the 3rd Chinese month (April 4 – May 4), the 6th Chinese month (July 7 – August 6), the 9th Chinese month (October 8 – November 6), and the 11th Chinese month (December 7, 2025 – January 4, 2026). Also, be careful about losing money, losing reputation, and contracting illnesses.

Health

For the health of young people this year, it is in good condition. With the power of youth and a prosperous career, there are good things that bring joy to the mind, helping physical and mental health. However, in the following months, you should take more care of your health because there is a chance of minor illnesses, such as the 3rd Chinese month (April 4 - May 4), the 6th Chinese month (July 7 - August 6), the 9th Chinese month (October 8 - November 6), and the 11th Chinese month (December 7, 2025 - January 4, 2026). In addition, you should be careful of accidents both during work and travel, and you should not drive while intoxicated.

For older people, be careful of the power of Tai-im that will affect your health, especially illnesses that come from eating whatever you want, whether it is eating sweet, salty, greasy food or food that is high in uric acid. Anyone who has any illness should avoid foods that are forbidden for that type of illness. You should also be careful of hidden diseases and slipping and falling that will cause injury.

Year of the OX (Fire) | (1949) & (2009)

"The OX in the barn" is a person born in the year of the OX at the age of 76 years (1949) and 15 years (2009)

Overview

For people in this age group, even though your business and career this year look bright on the outside, during the year, you cannot be confident. This is because many bad stars are appearing in your horoscope house. They will also cause you to have unstable emotions. It will make you feel irritated and annoyed with things around you easily. Please try to be calm and avoid interfering or controlling your family too much. Be careful of arguments. Be careful of accidents, especially water disasters. Be careful of health problems, such as gastritis, etc. However, you should control your diet and choose to eat only cleanly cooked food that is healthy. Avoid sweet, fatty, salty, and spicy food.

For teenagers, the planets transiting your horoscope house this year are the "Dao Tiang Kao" (Dao Dao Sap Tai) and the "Dao Sam Tai" (Dao Sam Kulbutr), which will bring both good and bad things. On the good side, they will help you be creative and increase your intelligence, which will lead to progress in your studies. Please be diligent and determined to study. You will not be disappointed. On the bad side, they will make you easily obsessed with one thing or another. And be careful of some friends who often persuade you to go astray, which will harm your future. Therefore, please be careful and always think and act with mindfulness.

Career and Business

For teenagers, even though their studies are progressing, they are influenced by many evil stars that are trying to block them. If they do whatever they want, they will be easily led astray. Therefore, they should keep their sanity and not be shaken by temptations or follow their invitations in the wrong way. If they know how to maintain their sanity, the auspicious star Sam Tai will appear to help them, helping their studies to be successful and progressive. In addition, starting a job or investing will have positive results.

The months in which both the career and education of the person in both cycles of life will change in a better direction are the 12th Chinese month (January 5 – February 2), the 2nd Chinese month (March 5 – April 3), the 7th Chinese month (August 7 – September 6), and the 10th Chinese month (November 7 – December 6). However, you should also be careful of the months in which your career will be obstructed and problematic, which are the 3rd Chinese month (April 4 – May 4), the 6th

Chinese month (July 7 – August 6), the 9th Chinese month (October 8 – November 6), and the 11th Chinese month (December 7, 2025 – January 4, 2026). During this period, be careful of being deceived by greed. When signing contracts, there is a chance of being at a disadvantage. Also, when starting a project or joint venture, be careful of problems and mistakes that may cause damage or loss.

Financial
The overall financial picture of both horoscopes this year is not very exciting. At times, there may be unexpected money passing through your hands to make you feel happy, but it is not prominent. Because when there is income, expenses will line up in a long line until you have almost no money to spend. Therefore, this year, be careful, whatever you can save, you should save first. Because if you spend money easily when there is income, you may run out of money later. This year, the months when your finances will be stuck and have problems, including unexpected expenses, are the 3rd Chinese month (April 4 - May 4), the 6th

Chinese month (July 7 - August 6), the 9th Chinese month (October 8 - November 6), and the 11th Chinese month (December 7, 2025 - January 4, 2026). Be careful of being tricked into investing and losing your money. Do not lend money to others. Do not sign financial guarantees. And do not be greedy for the benefits that others offer. The months when your finances will flow smoothly are the 12th Chinese month (January 5 – February 2), the 2nd Chinese month (March 5 – April 3), the 7th Chinese month (August 7 – September 6), and the 10th Chinese month (November 7 – December 6).

Family

This year, the family horoscope will have both good and bad things. Due to the influence of the Blue Dog Star and the Moon, it will cause inauspicious energy to cover and cause emotional damage. This year, be careful of arguments with family members or family members who have conflicts with neighbors and there will be a reason to lose money on medical expenses for family members. For teenagers this year, be careful of some friends with bad intentions who try to get close to you for some kind of gain. Both age groups must be very careful, especially during the unlucky months, which are the 3rd Chinese month (April 4 – May 4), the 6th Chinese month (July 7 – August 6), the 9th Chinese month (October 8 – November 6), and the 11th Chinese month (December 7, 2025 – January 4, 2026). Be careful of arguments in the home and arguments with outsiders. In any case, harmony and mutual understanding are always better than having problems.

Love

This year, love and relationships are not smooth. This is because of the influence of the evil stars that are focused on you, which can easily cause conflict, misunderstanding, and disagreement. It also makes you rash and emotional more than wise, so the results are often very bad. In particular, the months when your love life will easily experience problems and arguments are the 3rd Chinese month (April 4 – May 4), the 6th Chinese month (July

7 – August 6), the 9th Chinese month (October 8 – November 6), and the 11th Chinese month (December 7, 2025 – January 4, 2026). Be careful of conflicts that turn small matters into big ones. Be careful of a third party that may muddy the waters. Also, you should not go to entertainment or service establishments because you may end up in danger.

Health
For seniors, this year, health cannot be neglected. You should observe for abnormalities in your body and go for regular check-ups. Take medication as prescribed by the doctor. Be careful of dizziness and falls when walking. When traveling outside, find someone to take care of you.

For teenagers, health is not so good this year. Be careful of diseases caused by eating too much, food poisoning, gastritis, enteritis, and other diseases related to the stomach. In particular, the months when you should take special care of your health are the 3rd Chinese month (April 4 - May 4), the 6th Chinese month

(July 7 - August 6), the 9th Chinese month (October 8 - November 6), and the 11th Chinese month (December 7, 2025 - January 4, 2026). During work and travel, be careful of accidents. For teenagers, going out in groups may cause injury or you may suffer misfortune from something you did not do. Therefore, you should avoid it during these months.

Year of the OX (Earth) | (1961) (2021)

"The OX Journey" is a person born in the year of the OX at the age of 65 years (1961) and 15 years (2021)

Overview

For the senior horoscope around the age of 64, this year is another year that has many months in which the career and business are blessed by the auspicious stars shining and promoting smooth career and business as desired. However, there are some months in which the senior horoscope house is affected by the power of two stars, "Star Tiang Kao" (Blue Dog Star) and "Star Tai Im" (Moon Star), sending dark power covering the horoscope house, which will mainly affect health problems, especially diseases related to the digestive tract, including diseases caused by eating according to one's preferences, such as food poisoning, eating spicy, sweet, fatty, salty food in excess, gastroenteritis, etc., which will be the main cause of illness for the horoscope person. Therefore, you should take care of your health, find time to exercise lightly and be strict with yourself about eating.

For the horoscope person 4 years old, because the planets that orbit into the horoscope house this year are "Star Kiem Hong" (Star Sharp Sword) and "Star Sam Tai" (Star Three Sons) which shine together, which will cause the person to shine in terms of intelligence, cuteness, inquisitiveness, and curiosity about things around them. Moreover, a good memory helps with learning progress. However, when children have to travel far to strange places, parents should pay more attention and take closer care, especially regarding water because this year children are likely to be in danger from water. Therefore, they should be careful of water while traveling by boat, playing in ponds, rivers, canals, ponds or going to the sea, including danger from hot water scalds, so please take close care and be safe.

Career and Business

This year, the senior's work is considered to have a better direction than last year. The problems that used to cause you to worry, this year you will receive help from people around you. Even if there are obstacles, asking for cooperation from other parties will be smooth and convenient. Therefore, this year is a good opportunity for you to hurry up and continue the old work that is pending and push the work to be completed as soon as possible. The more diligent and persevering you are, the more results you will be able to create. You will be able to increase sales and income to gain more profit.

Especially during the months when your work is moving in a good direction and flourishing, namely the 12th Chinese month (January 5 - February 2), the 2nd Chinese month (March 5 - April 3), the 7th Chinese month (August 7 - September 6), and the 10th Chinese month (November 7 - December 6). During the months mentioned, you can choose to invest outside more because many channels have a good future and a bright direction. However, you should be careful during the bad months. Your work will be obstructed and face problems in the 3rd Chinese month (4 April - 4 May), the 6th Chinese month (7 July - 6 August), the 9th Chinese month (8 October - 6 November), and the 11th Chinese month (7 December 2025 - 4 January 2026) in which you should avoid interfering in other people's work duties, especially avoiding getting involved in other people's legal cases. When signing work contracts, you should check the details in the contract. Do not sign reliably without checking or problems will arise later.

Financial

This year, seniors will have abundant financial fortunes. They will receive income from many channels. Furthermore, their investments will yield expected returns. In particular, the months when their finances will flow smoothly are the 12th Chinese month (January 5 – February 2), the 2nd Chinese month (March 5 – April 3), the 7th Chinese month (August 7 – September 6), and the 10th Chinese month (November 7 – December 6). The months when their finances will be problematic and seniors should be careful of unexpected expenses are the 3rd Chinese month (April 4 – May 4), the 6th Chinese month (July 7 – August 6), the 9th Chinese month (October 8 – November 6), and the 11th Chinese month (December 7, 2025 – January 4, 2026). You should not lend money to others, not sign financial guarantees, and should avoid gambling and risking your luck. You should also not invest or get involved in illegal businesses.

Family

This year, due to the auspicious stars shining the way, the family of the person will receive auspicious power. In your house this year, there is a chance to organize an auspicious event for your children, whether it is an engagement ceremony or a wedding ceremony, or your daughter or daughter-in-law will give birth to a child for you to admire. Otherwise, the person has a chance to buy expensive property for the house or move into a new house. However, this year, there are some months that you should be careful of that problems will occur within the family, namely the 3rd Chinese month (April 4 - May 4), the 6th Chinese month (July 7 - August 6), the 9th Chinese month (October 8 - November 6), and the 11th Chinese month (December 7, 2025 - January 4, 2026). You should be careful of losing valuables, be careful of scammers, be careful of family members who get injured and bleed, and be careful of arguments both inside and outside the house. In addition, you should not get involved in conflicts between friends. Be careful of misfortunes.

Love

This year, your relationship with your senior spouse may not be as you wish. Whatever you talk about or express your opinions to each other, they may become different stories and go in different directions. Opinions tend to disagree easily. In any case, please be patient and calm. Also, you should not interfere or interfere in other people's family matters. Avoid hanging out at entertainment venues that offer services because in addition to losing money, be careful that it will ruin your reputation by catching an illness as a bonus. The person should be careful during the following months: the 3rd Chinese month (April 4 - May 4), the 6th Chinese month (July 7 - August 6), the 9th Chinese month (October 8 - November 6), and the 11th Chinese month (December 7, 2025 - January 4, 2026).

Health

This year, the health of the elderly is not so good. You should take good care of yourself. If you work too hard and do not get enough rest, your life, eating and living are sloppy. Just to get through it will become a hidden disease that threatens you. You should be careful of back pain, waist pain, gastritis, and intestinal inflammation. Your old illnesses will flare up, especially during the months when you need to take close care of your health, which are the 3rd Chinese month (April 4 – May 4), the 6th Chinese month (July 7 – August 6), the 9th Chinese month (October 8 – November 6), and the 11th Chinese month (December 7, 2025 – January 4, 2026). In addition, during these times, you must be careful of accidents both while working and traveling. Be careful of food that is toxic and can cause other illnesses to flare up. For young children, parents should be careful of accidents that may happen to them during these months.

Year of the OX (Wood) | (1971)

" The OX plowing the fields" is a person born in the year of the OX at the age of 52 years (1971)

Overview

For the Ox horoscope in this age group, this year will be another year that the horoscope house will find many auspicious stars orbiting to support, which will promote the opportunity for your home to organize auspicious and joyful events, whether it is a birthday party, housewarming party, or a party to welcome a new family member or a wedding ceremony for children. There will also be an opportunity to buy expensive property, an opportunity to move into a new house. The direction of work and trade will be bright and prosperous. In addition, both internal and external investments are bright. The expected dividends are likely to be received as desired. However, during the year, there will be a group of inauspicious stars orbiting to destroy and harass the horoscope house, which are the evil stars "Guangji" (tongue-rolling star), "Kiem Hong" (sharp sword star), and "Tai Yim" (moon star), all of which will have an impact on arguments, conflicts, problems, and obstacles in work. Trade and sales will be fiercely competitive. It will also affect the safety and well-being of family members. Therefore, to carry out any work activities this year, you must assess your potential in terms of capital, ability, and manpower for management, including keeping the truth in trade. This year you must be careful that if you can't do as you say, the credit you have built up for a long time will be lost, causing damage to your work and ruining your reputation.

Career and Business

This year's career or business shows a path of progress. This year is suitable for creating work, expanding work, increasing production, adding branches, or finding ways to expand income in various areas. Or increasing investment will all receive positive feedback. In particular, you should strike while the fire is hot in the months when your career and business are smooth and prosperous, namely the 12th Chinese month (January 5 - February 2), the 2nd Chinese month (March 5 - April 3), the 7th Chinese month (August 7 - September 6), and the 10th Chinese month (November 7 - December 6). However, during the aforementioned period, you should be careful not to use emotions to create conflicts that will negatively affect your work. In addition, if you have to sign a work contract, you should carefully check the details in the contract. In particular, the months when your work will be easily hindered and have problems include the 3rd Chinese month (4 April - 4 May), the 6th Chinese month (7 July - 6 August), the 9th Chinese month (8 October - 6 November), and the 11th Chinese month (7 December 2025 - 4 January 2026). Investing in various matters during these times is very risky. You should also be careful of problems with funds that will affect your work. Beware of dishonest people. Frequently go in and check the accounting system and the management of people and stock.

Financial

This year, even though your finances are stable and not a problem for you, the word "good income" does not mean that you will have money piled up in front of you. The income that flows in must come from diligence and dedication to making a living. This includes various investments, whether it is your own business or investing in the stock market, money market, or gold market. If you enter and exit at the right time, you will become very rich. Especially during the months when your finances are prosperous and have good liquidity, namely the 12th Chinese month (January 5 – February 2), the 2nd Chinese month (March 5 – April 3), the 7th Chinese month (August 7 – September 6), and the 10th Chinese month (November 7 – December 6). However, since there are some months during the year when your financial star is low, you need to manage your liquidity well. Be careful that your cash flow does not get stuck. Therefore, save anything you can save first so that you do not fall into a crisis. In particular, the months when you must be careful about unexpected expenses are the 3rd Chinese month (4 April - 4 May), the 6th Chinese month (7 July - 6 August), the 9th Chinese month (8 October - 6 November), and the 11th Chinese month (7 December 2025 - 4 January 2026) when it is forbidden to lend money to others, to be a financial guarantee, to gamble and take risks, and to invest in illegal businesses.

Family

This year, the family aspect of this horoscope has both good and bad things mixed. That is, during the year, you will receive good news that will make you happy and there may be auspicious events in the house that will make you happy. There is a chance to move into a new house or have new family members. There will also be an opportunity to buy expensive property. But on the other hand, there will be unexpected events that will affect you. Beware of relatives or friends who will backstab you and cause you damage and suffering. Especially in the following months, there will be problems and unrest in the family, which are the 3rd Chinese month (April 4 - May 4), the 6th

Chinese month (July 7 - August 6), the 9th Chinese month (October 8 - November 6), and the 11th Chinese month (December 7, 2025 - January 4, 2026). During these periods, beware of accidents that may happen to family members, arguments, and quarrels both inside and outside the house, and beware of dangers from criminals.

Love
This year, the love destiny of this age group is in good condition. Although there may be some conflicts and arguments, you will be able to understand each other. There will also be an opportunity to go on a long journey together, whether it is to make merit, visit relatives who live far away or go on a trip together. However, you should be careful during the months when your love is quite fragile and arguments can easily occur, which are the 3rd Chinese month (April 4 – May 4), the 6th Chinese month (July 7 – August 6), the 9th Chinese month (October 8 – November 6), and the 11th Chinese month (December 7, 2025 – January 4, 2026). Please control yourself and travel mindfully. Also, you

should not interfere in other people's family matters.

Health

This year, the health of the person is considered moderate. You should get enough sleep and exercise to strengthen your immune system. Avoid eating cold foods such as winter melon, cucumber, watermelon, etc. and cold foods. You should also be careful of gastritis, enteritis, and food poisoning. In particular, the months when you should take care of your health more are the 3rd Chinese month (April 4 – May 4), the 6th Chinese month (July 7 – August 6), the 9th Chinese month (October 8 – November 6), and the 11th Chinese month (December 7, 2025 – January 4, 2026). In addition, you should be careful of accidents both while traveling and at work. If you have to go to a party or social gathering where alcohol is consumed, you should avoid driving.

Year of the OX (Wood) | (1985)

" The OX in the Sea" is a person born in the year of the OX at the age of 40 years (1985)

Overview

For the Ox people in this age group, this year is a year that you cannot be hasty. Everything requires mindfulness and patience. Look carefully and comprehensively before taking any steps. You must maintain diligence and perseverance in learning and developing yourself to be able to successfully reach your goal. You must also be careful because the horoscope also appears with negative energy, which has the influence to easily cause accidents during work and travel. You should be careful in your life and take care of your love life. Avoid going to entertainment venues that are hidden in selling services to create peace within your family because living together as a couple means living together with love and sincerity. When the family is harmonious, peace will arise. However, you are still lucky that this year in the horoscope, there is an auspicious star of happiness and fortune that will orbit and visit you. This will spread its influence and affect the prosperity of your career or business, which will have a clear and pleasant direction of progress. It encourages people who do not have their own business yet. This year, they will have the opportunity to build themselves up and have a business that is as they wish. Some people will have the opportunity to merge their businesses to be bigger or have new channels for investment. These are all bright future paths waiting for you.

Career and Business

This year is another year that your career will clearly show its prosperity. You will have the opportunity to expand your business and create achievements, but the condition is that you must be determined and find a way to improve your skills to keep up with the changes. If you are looking for an assistant this year, it is not against the rules. Try to find someone with a good heart to work with you, and they will help you continue your big project successfully. The months in which your career will show a good direction of progress and prosperity are the 12th Chinese month (January 5 – February 2), the 2nd Chinese month (March 5 – April 3), the 7th Chinese month (August 7 – September 6), and the 10th Chinese month (November 7 – December 6). In addition, during this period, joint ventures, starting new projects, or investing in expanding your business in various matters can all be done. The direction is good, but you should still assess your financial resources so that you can continuously invest. If you calculate and find that you are too liquid to borrow money and have a large debt, it would not be suitable. The months when your work will be obstructed and face problems are the 3rd Chinese month (April 4 - May 4), the 6th Chinese month (July 7 - August 6), the 9th Chinese month (October 8 - November 6), and the 11th Chinese month (December 7, 2025 - January 4, 2026). Be careful of falling into traps and being tricked by criminals. Also, be careful of errors in the accounting system. Signing an employment contract or accepting work should be reviewed carefully because it could lead to disadvantages and cause you problems later.

Financial

This year, your finances are not stable. Therefore, you should save and save some reserve money for your expenses. You must also manage and maintain liquidity. When investing in a large sum of money, you should consider the working capital capacity to be able to continuously circulate or not. If you do not have reserve money or a reliable source of loans, it is necessary to postpone the project. It is better than rushing to do it and causing you to face a crisis in the middle. In addition, trading and investing that is risky or violates morality and the law of the country should not be done, especially during the months when your financial star is low. Be careful of unexpected expenses, such as the 3rd Chinese month (April 4 - May 4), the 6th Chinese month (July 7 - August 6), the 9th Chinese month (October 8 - November 6), and the 11th Chinese month (December 7, 2025 - January 4, 2026). Do not lend money, sign guarantees, or make contracts. Do not gamble. The months when your finances will flow smoothly are the 12th Chinese month (January 5 – February 2), the 2nd Chinese month (March 5 – April 3), the 7th Chinese month (August 7 – September 6), and the 10th Chinese month (November 7 – December 6).

Family

This year, due to the auspicious energy visiting the house, during the year, the person will likely buy expensive property. There will be an opportunity to move into a new house or residence. However, what you should be careful about is that there will be arguments with neighbors, which may lead to various incidents, especially during the months when problems and conflicts within the family can easily arise, namely the 3rd Chinese month (April 4 – May 4), the 6th Chinese month (July 7 – August 6), the 9th Chinese month (October 8 – November 6), and the 11th Chinese month (December 7, 2025 – January 4, 2026). Be careful of arguments within the family or people in the house having problems with neighbors. Be careful of losing valuables and falling victim to fraud.

Love

This year, your love life will not be smooth at times, but if you dare to do, dare to accept, dare to apologize, your lover will be happy to forgive you. Especially during the months when your love life will be easily plagued with problems and arguments, namely the 3rd Chinese month (April 4 - May 4), the 6th Chinese month (July 7 - August 6), the 9th Chinese month (October 8 - November 6), and the 11th Chinese month (December 7, 2025 - January 4, 2026). During these times, you should not interfere in other people's family matters. Do not go to entertainment venues that offer services. Beware of illnesses and arguments that will follow.

Health

This year's overall health is moderate. The important thing is to be careful about cirrhosis of the liver or problems from drinking too much alcohol. In addition, you should take care of your eating and living hygiene. Be careful of gastritis, enteritis, and food poisoning, and avoid eating foods with cold elements or cold foods. The months when you should take close care of your health are the 3rd Chinese month (April 4 - May 4), the 6th Chinese month (July 7 - August 6), the 9th Chinese month (October 8 - November 6), and the 11th Chinese month (December 7, 2025 - January 4, 2026). In addition, you should be careful of accidents both at work and while traveling that may cause bloodshed. After a party where you drink alcohol, you should not drive. Be careful about the cleanliness of your food. Reduce spicy foods and find free time to exercise to strengthen your health.

Chinese Astrology Horoscope for Each Month

Month 12 in the Dragon Year (5 Jan 25 - 2 Feb 25)
This month marks the beginning of the Chinese New Year, which is considered an auspicious month for the Ox. Overall, life will be smooth. Your career and business will progress, and you will be able to expand, create new works, or branch out, or you will have new interesting channels for trade and investment. However, you should not be too complacent with your work progress. Instead, you should take this opportunity to analyze your work in the past year to see what are the shortcomings that should be fixed, and what should be added or adjusted to keep up with the ever-changing changes. You should also prepare both your people and tools, cover your weaknesses, and strengthen your strengths. Dare to try different things, and most importantly, you must constantly seek knowledge and develop yourself. Then you will be able to see the results of your prosperity tangibly and brightly.

In addition, you should always build and strengthen good relationships with your colleagues and those close to you. Your financial fortune this month is normal, but there are obstacles. You will find someone to help you. You are also likely to receive money from fortune, but since there is not much, do not spend too much, including extra money in things you invest in. As for your work or investments, during this period you will receive satisfactory returns, but you should still spend sparingly and always save money.

Your family is prosperous and happy. In terms of love, If you still act like a kangaroo, you won't want to seriously date anyone. During this time, you should avoid going to entertainment venues. Be careful of getting extras. In terms of health, you are healthy and have no problems.

Support Days: 4 Jan., 8 Jan., 12 Jan., 16 Jan., 20 Jan., 24 Jan., 28 Jan.
Lucky Days: 7 Jan., 19 Jan., 31 Jan.
Misfortune Days: 2 Jan., 14 Jan., 26 Jan.
Bad Days: 1 Jan., 11 Jan., 13 Jan., 23 Jan., 25 Jan.

Month 1 in the Snake Year (3 Feb 25 - 4 Mar 25)
This month, for the Ox, your horoscope seems to be blocked by a force, making it easy to lose money. An easy way to solve this problem is to make merit at the beginning of the month, which will help ease the burden. At this time, the most important thing you should do is to do good deeds, make merit, and follow the precepts.

Your career is in a situation where people tend to cause trouble. You should be patient and calm, and avoid responding violently. In addition, there will be many things coming up in your work and business during this period. You have to make a decision carefully because if you choose the wrong path, be careful or you will lose everything. However, during this period, visiting your customers to strengthen your relationship will help you overcome the crisis quite a bit.

As for the direction of various investments, it is not bright during this period. This month, your financial luck will be smooth. However, the money from luck is very risky. Therefore, if you can avoid investing, you will not get hurt. Because during this period, you will be in danger of losing money. Therefore, you should avoid lending money to others or signing guarantees for anyone.

Your family is not peaceful. Be careful that someone will cause trouble and cause damage. But your love life is so smooth and sweet that people around you will be jealous. Your health is good, but you should avoid eating raw food, which is risky and can lead to illnesses.

Support Days: 1 Feb., 5 Feb., 9 Feb., 13 Feb., 17 Feb., 21 Feb., 25 Feb.
Lucky Days: 12 Feb., 24 Feb.
Misfortune Days: 7 Feb., 19 Feb.
Bad Days: 4 Feb., 6 Feb., 16 Feb., 18 Feb., 28 Feb.

Month 2 in the Snake Year (5 Mar 25 – 3 Apr 25)
This month, the life path of the person will receive the support of the partner month, as well as the auspicious power from the good stars, making the work and business smooth and prosperous, with obvious progress. In addition, you will find someone to help you solve your worries. Therefore, you should seize and use this good opportunity to check your readiness in all aspects to prepare to move to pioneer new channels expand your business, create work, or start investing again.

Your financial fortune during this period will have cash flow in two ways: direct from regular income and sales, special income from special work, and windfall money. You will have to manage and divide your investment, spending, and savings well to use the money to the maximum benefit.

In terms of family, there will be good news about auspicious work. Love is a time when love trees produce satisfactory results. Your lover takes care of you and pays attention to you closely. Therefore, you should cherish this time. As for relatives and friends, be careful of jealous people. You have to be careful with your words. Do not brag or boast too much or you will be envied. And refrain from gossiping about other people.

In terms of health, during this period, there is a chance of deterioration due to working too hard and not getting enough rest. You should also be careful of gastritis and avoid eating foods that make your body feel cold.

Support Days: 1 Mar., 5 Mar., 9 Mar., 13 Mar., 17 Mar., 21 Mar., 25 Mar., 29 Mar.
Lucky Days: 8 Mar., 20 Mar.
Misfortune Days: 3 Mar., 15 Mar., 27 Mar.
Bad Days: 2 Mar., 12 Mar., 14 Mar., 24 Mar., 26 Mar.

Month 3 in the Snake Year (4 Apr 25 - 4 May 25)
This month, your horoscope has moved to the destroyer line. It is also affected by the evil star "Xiao Ae" (the destroyer) that is orbiting and focusing on your horoscope house. This will cause your work and business to encounter many obstacles and problems during this period. You will have to be in a state of submission and pressure. It is also easy to have conflicts with your colleagues. Therefore, you should adjust yourself and find a way to manage your work well. This month, you need to be more careful when signing contracts and doing any legal transactions. You should not be greedy for the benefits that do not belong to you. The most important thing you should do this month is to support yourself and take care of your work and responsibilities as best you can. Do not act so prominently that people around you will feel annoyed. You must also maintain good relationships with people you have to contact at both the upper and lower levels. That is, being able to reach your boss and understand your subordinates will help you get through this.

This month, your finances will encounter a storm. You will have to spend more money than you earn. Your cash flow will be stuck and liquid for almost the entire month. In addition, you should be careful about bad debts in your debtor account during this period. You should manage your money closely. Starting a new job and investing in various things are not good. There is a chance that you will be cheated.

In this period of family fate, you should be careful of accidents that may cause family members to be injured to the point of bleeding. Be careful of elders getting sick or unexpected events. Relatives should stay away.

Love is not yet peaceful. There will always be things that cause conflict. The person with this fate should try to adjust their emotions and reduce their stubbornness. Face each other and talk to each other with reason.

Health during this period will be easy to get sick. You should take good care of your health.

You should exercise regularly and eat healthy food.

Support Days: 2 Apr., 6 Apr., 10 Apr., 14 Apr., 18 Apr., 22 Apr., 26 Apr., 30 Apr.
Lucky Days: 1 Apr., 13 Apr., 25 Apr.
Misfortune Days: 8 Apr., 20 Apr.
Bad Days: 5 Apr., 7 Apr., 17 Apr., 19 Apr., 29 Apr.

Month 4 in the Snake Year (5 May 25 - 4 Jun 25)
This month, your fate is quite volatile due to the influence of the evil stars that are harassing you, causing your mind to be quite scattered and scattered. When making a decision, you do not dare to make a decision. You hesitate and think over and over again, but cannot find a conclusion on which way to go. For your work and business, this month, please do your best and keep your mind as steady as a mountain. No matter who tries to persuade you about anything, please stand by the information you have and go all the way. The important thing is that your actions and activities must be honest

to be successful. In addition, there is something you should do during this period: dare to be clear and decisive.

Do not let yourself be the head of a tiger and the tail of a snake like a monster that is not in tune. This will cause work to be delayed and difficult to complete.

However, in terms of luck and finances, things are bright. There is an opportunity to reap the benefits from what you have invested and worked hard in the past. There is also a chance that you will be successful and receive a windfall. However, you should also save up at the same time. As for your work or investments, this period is good and will bring back satisfying returns.

In terms of family, it is peaceful. If there are any obstacles, you will find a patron to help. There is a chance that you will buy expensive property or move into a new house. Relatives will help you and have the opportunity to do public service together or do charity work.

Even though your love relationship looks sweeter, you still need to spend time together to add sweetness. Don't let yourself miss out on buying gifts and souvenirs, and maintain consistency. Then your love will be beautiful and long-lasting.

Your health is strong and you are full of energy, but don't be careless and exercise regularly.

Support Days: 4 May, 8 May., 12 May., 16 May., 20 May., 24 May., 28 May.
Lucky Days: 7 May., 19 May., 31 May.
Misfortune Days: 2 May, 14 May., 26 May.
Bad Days: 1 May, 11 May., 13 May., 23 May., 25 May.

Month 5 in the Snake Year (5 Jun 25 - 6 Jul 25)
This month, the direction of your horoscope for those born in the year of the Ox is on an upward trend. Your career and business are still on the path of prosperity. However, your horoscope cannot escape the influence of the evil forces that are harassing you. Therefore, you cannot

be careless. Every activity should be considered with prudence and gradually solve problems in order of importance because the bad things are almost over. Do not be impatient or do anything rashly. You should use good human relations skills to contact and do business. This will bring good results for yourself and your work. As for working together or investing, this opportunity is possible. There will be a fair amount of dividends, but you should not devote too much.

In terms of fortune, you will have a good amount of income. Your finances are quite good, flowing in from many channels. There will be money from your fortune passing through your hands, making you spend more easily. However, you cannot be too extravagant because unexpected expenses will occur. Therefore, you should always save money for emergencies so that you will not be in need.

In terms of family, during this period, you must closely take care of the health of the elderly in the house. Be careful not to have an unexpected accident or a chronic disease flare-up. Relatives and friends should stay away from you for a while. In addition, words that cannot be revealed completely will be a threat that will come back to haunt you later.

In terms of love, you are moderately happy and cheerful. Overall, it is still okay, but be careful that being attracted to service girls will bring you trouble.

In terms of health, you are quite healthy, but you should exercise regularly.

Support Days: 1 Jun., 5 Jun., 9 Jun., 13 Jun., 17 Jun., 21 Jun., 25 Jun., 29 Jun.
Lucky Days: 12 Jun., 24 Jun.
Misfortune Days: 7 Jun., 19 Jun.
Bad Days: 4 Jun., 6 Jun., 16 Jun., 18 Jun., 28 Jun., 30 Jun.

Month 6 in the Snake Year (7 Jul 25 - 6 Aug 25)

This month, your life path will encounter a storm, and your fate will fall and plummet. There will be irregularities in every aspect. During this period, the thing that causes the most stress and suffering is:

Problems of conflict between individuals, if you can just be patient, you will be able to overcome the crisis. What you should do at this time is sometimes you may have to compromise a little, rather than rushing into it and causing both of you to break up. As for your work or investment, it is not going well, so you should postpone it for now.

In terms of finances, you will encounter a storm. You should closely monitor the liquidity of your working capital. Cut out unnecessary expenses to maintain some money in the system.

Do not lend money to people close to you or guarantee for others. Do not gamble or invest in illegal businesses because you may encounter bad luck to the point of being imprisoned.

As for your family, your fate is not smooth. During this period, there is a possibility of spending money on medical expenses for family members. Relatives and friends during this period will bring trouble or problems, so you should keep your distance and not indulge your friends or they will cause you even more trouble.

In terms of love, it is still a period of strife. You should find time to adjust your understanding and talk things out. Think back to when you were first in love.

In terms of health, your physical health is not good either. Be careful of colds and allergies, and when traveling near or far, be extra careful of accidents.

Support Days: 3 Jul., 7 Jul., 11 Jul., 15 Jul., 19 Jul., 23 Jul., 27 Jul., 31 Jul.
Lucky Days: 6 Jul., 18 Jul., 30 Jul.

Misfortune Days: 1 Jul., 13 Jul., 25 Jul.
Bad Days: 10 Jul., 12 Jul., 22 Jul., 24 Jul.

Month 7 in the Snake Year (7 Aug 25 - 6 Sep 25)

This month, the horoscope moves to a friendly month. Although major problems and obstacles will be resolved by a sponsor, conflicts between individuals remain. Therefore, your career and business still need to be well-established and take care of your responsibilities as best you can. When you are still struggling to survive, do not interfere in others' work. What you should do on this occasion is to know how to publicize your abilities, but do not be too forward in an ugly way. This will help restore your good image.

This month, your main income from direct work will grow and increase. As for windfall money, you will have some, but you should assess the amount of income and expenditure to see if it is worth investing in. Investing in shares, starting a new job, or choosing to invest in new businesses will have good results.

There is peace within the family. Relatives will be the sponsors.

Love horoscope shows more understanding and compromise with each other.

In terms of health, even though there are no serious illnesses to be alarmed about during this period, you should pay attention to your living conditions, eating, and getting enough sleep. If your body is tired, it will cause your efficiency to decline and accidents may occur. During this time, it may lead to injuries, bleeding, and danger.

Support Days: 4 Aug., 8 Aug., 12 Aug., 16 Aug., 20 Aug., 24 Aug., 28 Aug.
Lucky Days: 11 Aug., 23 Aug.
Misfortune Days: 6 Aug., 18 Aug., 30 Aug.
Bad Days: 3 Aug., 5 Aug., 15 Aug., 17 Aug., 27 Aug., 29 Aug.

Month 8 in the Snake Year (7 Sep 25 - 7 Oct 25)

This month, those born in the year of the Ox will still receive the power of the auspicious star, which will help your career progress and your business flourish. What you hope for and intend to do during this period will be as successful as you wish. What you should do this month is to push forward the project or project that you planned or do something that you have planned but have not had the opportunity to do. This period is a good opportunity for you to accelerate as you wish, but you should do it under readiness in terms of budget, management, and time. Because if you still hesitate and do not dare to make a decision, the good opportunity that comes during this period may pass you by.

This month, your financial luck will be abundant. Whatever you touch will seem to turn into money as you wish. Joint ventures, starting a new job, buying shares, and short-term investments, this period has a bright direction. There will be pleasing dividends. Therefore, you should not let time go to waste.

Your family will be peaceful and smooth. Many things will be as you wish. Regarding close relatives and friends, even though there may be disagreements on some matters, the conclusion is that both parties will be accepted.

In terms of love, this period is auspicious. For some couples who have been dating for a while, this period is a good time to propose or get married. Or some people this month have a chance to welcome a new little family member.

In terms of health, you will be healthy during this period, so there is no need to worry because when you are comfortable and happy, illnesses will not come to bother you.

Support Days: 1 Sep, 5 Sep., 9 Sep., 13 Sep., 17 Sep., 21 Sep., 25 Sep., 29 Sep.
Lucky Days: 4 Sep, 16 Sep., 28 Sep.
Misfortune Days: 11 Sep, 23 Sep.,
Bad Days: 8 Sep, 10 Sep., 20 Sep., 22 Sep.

Month 9 in the Snake Year (8 Oct 25 - 6 Nov 25)
This month, for those born in the year of the
Ox, is a period of vigilance. You must always
listen to external events and know how to
adapt and change. If you can attack, do it. If
you can't, wait. Being hasty and going back will
only make things go to waste. What you
should do now is to constantly build and
strengthen relationships with people you have
to deal with regularly, such as your superiors,
subordinates, colleagues, customers, and
business partners, to wait for the right time
when opportunities open up before moving
forward again. Your work and business will be
smooth and without obstacles.

Your finances this month are average.
Although your direct income is good, you must
be careful about money from unexpected
gambling and gambling. Don't be greedy or it
will cause you losses. Always have a careful
spending plan.

In terms of your work, during this period,
strengthening your relationships with people

will also benefit you. This will result in supporters who will help your work and business go smoothly. Therefore, you should be very diligent. The more you do, the more you will make money. You should be careful about joint ventures, starting new jobs, and investing in various areas during this period. You will encounter problems with the liquidity of funds and accounting system problems. Also, be careful of people who are dishonest and cause damage.

In terms of your family, be careful of your subordinates or servants in the house causing trouble. Increase your caution from scammers.

In terms of love, you should not interfere in other people's lives. Take time to take care of your lover. During this period, be careful about looking for extras outside the home, as it will bring danger.

In terms of health, the person is healthy.

Support Days: 3 Oct., 7 Oct., 11 Oct., 15 Oct., 19 Oct., 23 Oct., 27 Oct., 31 Oct.
Lucky Days: 10 Oct., 22 Oct.
Misfortune Days: 5 Oct., 17 Oct., 29 Oct.
Bad Days: 2 Oct., 4 Oct., 14 Oct., 16 Oct., 26 Oct., 28 Oct.

Month 10 in the Snake Year (7 Nov 25 - 6 Dec 25)
This month, your horoscope shows auspicious stars shining, which will make your career, business, and family life better. Please be determined and develop yourself continuously. Progress will appear. However, the important thing is that when you are doing well, do not forget yourself and act arrogantly. This will destroy your future. This year, please use respect and humility. It will be more beneficial to you. What you should do this month is seize the moment when your luck is rising. Strike while the iron is hot by finding new investment channels to make money grow. This will create results, increase production, or accelerate sales.

Although your financial horoscope is moderate, this month you will have a chance to get lucky, which will bring unexpected additional income. As for direct cash flow, there will be some.
If you do not choose to invest in risky or illegal activities, you will see a beautiful balance in your account. This month, your investment will have a bright direction.

In terms of family, you will receive auspicious energy. You will receive good news, which may be an auspicious job or the success of your family members or relatives. During this time, you will have the opportunity to join in doing good deeds for society or join in a charity event together.

In terms of love, it is sweet. Lovers or spouses will take care of each other and stick together. The love tree will grow and bloom to welcome the bright end of the year. In addition, health will be strong and supportive of work and money.

Support Days: 4 Nov., 8 Nov., 12 Nov., 16 Nov., 20 Nov., 24 Nov., 28 Nov.
Lucky Days: 3 Nov., 15 Nov., 27 Nov.
Misfortune Days: 10 Nov., 22 Nov.
Bad Days: 7 Nov., 9 Nov., 19 Nov., 21 Nov.

Month 11 in the Snake Year (7 Dec 25 - 4 Jan 25)
This month, your horoscope will encounter storms, causing you to face obstacles and problems and have the opportunity to suffer in every aspect, especially in signing contracts related to work. You should check carefully and be careful of subordinates causing trouble. You should look at every activity and thoroughly check information before doing anything to prevent mistakes. What you should do this month is to have compassion and help others. If you have the opportunity to show kindness and help others without causing yourself any trouble, you should do it. It is considered a good deed that will not be lost.

This month, your finances lack liquidity. In addition to being careful of unexpected large expenses that may interfere, you should not be greedy for money that you do not deserve because you may encounter lawsuits. You should also stay away from gambling and risky investments in risky businesses. You must be strict about saving and always manage your spending to maintain a balance.

During this period, your family lacks peace. Be careful of accidents that may happen to family members. Relatives should not interfere or interfere in other people's matters.

In terms of love, it is smooth. This month is another month with a good time for asking for a proposal, getting engaged, or getting married.

However, health is not good. Be careful of high blood pressure, heart disease, and clogged arteries. Including increasing caution against accidents both while working and traveling.

Support Days: 2 Dec., 6 Dec., 10 Dec., 14 Dec., 18 Dec., 22 Dec., 26 Dec., 30 Dec.

Lucky Days: 9 Dec., 21 Dec.

Misfortune Days: 4 Dec., 16 Dec., 28 Dec.

Bad Days: 1 Dec., 3 Dec., 13 Dec., 15 Dec., 25 Dec., 27 Dec.

Amulet for The Year of the OX
"Tang Sanzang saves animals"

Those born in the year of the Ox this year should set up and worship the sacred object "Tang Sanzang, the Prophet of Animals" to enhance their fortune. Place it on your work desk or cash desk to ask for his power and authority to protect you from dangers, eliminate bad things and dangers that will affect you this year, and make them disappear. Ask for his blessing to help support you with good fortune, happiness, and prosperity with wealth and fortune, and bring peace and happiness to you.

In a chapter on advanced Feng Shui, it is mentioned that the deities who will come down to reside in the Mie Keng (house of destiny) of the year, are deities who can bring both good and bad fortune to you. Therefore, worshiping to enhance your fortune with a deity who comes down to reside in your birth year is considered to have the best results and the most impact on you. This is to rely on the power of that deity to help protect you while your fortune is declining and having bad luck to alleviate it. At the same time, ask for his blessing to help your business and trade run smoothly as you wish. Bring glory to you and your family.

For those born in the year of the Ox or Mie Keng (horoscope house) in the zodiac sign Tiu, this year is an auspicious year with good fortune for you. Your career has a chance to advance. You have a chance to expand your business. Even though you will struggle hard, you will have a satisfactory income. External investments are bright and will return good numbers.

This year, for those who work for a salary, it is a good time to change jobs and seek better opportunities. However, during the year, there will be an inauspicious constellation moving into the horoscope house, which are all stars that will affect arguments, conflicts, problems, and obstacles in your work. Trade and sales will be fiercely competitive. It will affect the safety and well-being of your family members and you may be deceived by ill-wishers. Beware of dangers from water.

For health, beware of accidents that will cause you to be injured, bleed, and stray bullets from arguments. In particular, Ox horoscopes around the age of 64 should be careful of losing their property.

Love relationships are not smooth this year, so it is normal for you to feel more lonely. Therefore, if you want to promote and increase the auspicious things to have clear results, you should set up and worship "Phra Tang Sanzang, the Animal Lover" to ask for his power to help eliminate all serious disasters and disasters, create more auspicious wealth, and make your business and career progress as you wish. "Phra Dharma Master Tang Sanzang" was originally named "Xianzang, Surname Tan". He was from Henan Province, China. He was a genius by birth. He was someone who studied the Dharma since he was young. When he grew up, he became a monk and was famous for his morality, meditation, and wisdom. He was supported by Emperor Tang Taizong, the first emperor of the Tang Dynasty. Emperor Tang Taizong was a person who highly admired Buddhism and loved and respected Phra Xianzang very much. Therefore, he made him his adopted younger brother. Phra Xianzang was a diligent monk who devoted his life to worshiping the Buddha by studying, researching, and collecting the true teachings of Buddhism. Traveling from China to the remote and rugged land of Jambudvipa, took 19 years and covered a distance of more than 50,000 li. He was determined to spread Buddhism and collect the Tripitaka, which was of great benefit to the people of the world. Therefore, he was given the name "Tang Sanzang", which means "Tripitaka". The Chinese called him "Tang Sanzang Huabsi", which means "The Dharma Master who translated the Tripitaka in the Tang Dynasty". Worshiping the Buddha will help eliminate disasters, misfortunes, and sorrows, eliminate evil people who cause trouble, and find a convenient and bright path in doing business and various duties. It also helps everything to go smoothly as desired.

In addition, those born in the year of the Ox should wear a lucky pendant of "Tang Sanzang, the Buddha who saves animals" around their necks or carry it with them when traveling both near and far from home, so that the person will be filled with auspicious treasures and places, have prosperity and progress in both business and trade, and have a peaceful and happy family throughout the year, resulting in better and faster efficiency and effectiveness than before.

Good Direction: Northeast, Southeast, and North
Bad Direction: Southwest
Lucky Colors: Red, Pink, Orange, Cream, and Yellow
Lucky Times: 09.00 - 10.59, 17.00 - 18.59, 25.00 - 00.59.
Bad Times: 11.00 – 11.59, 13.00 – 14.59, 19.00 – 20.59.

Good Luck For 2025